Randomly Accessed Poetics

Issue No. 4
Heart Splatters Into Significance

Penhead Press

Features
Washington Writers & Artists

Cover Design
W. J. Lindberg

Editor
W.J. Lindberg

Randomly Accessed Poetics

Issue 4: Heart Splatters Into Significance
Featuring Washington Writers & Artists
Edition Number Two (1st Print Edition), March 2014

ISBN: 978-0-9887938-2-8

Randomly Accessed Poetics™ has prior written permission from each of the respective authors to print or reprint the works contained in this Literary Collection.

All individual works contained herein are copyright © 2014 by their respective authors, unless otherwise indicated.

Reprints or Previously Published Works *(this includes pieces published on rapoetics.com, randomly-accessed-poetics.com, penhead-press.com, an individual author's personal blog, print and online literary journals, or (handmade) self-publications):*

Lunch at What Was Once the Depot, © 2013 by Jim Davis
The Agony of Love © 2013 by William Wright Harris
The Mirage © 2013 by Dawnell Harrison
Grit © 2013 by Scott Laudati
The Sermon © 2010 by Carol Smallwood

All rights reserved.

No part of this publication may be reproduced, stored in a retrieval system, or transmitted in any form or by any means, electronic, mechanically printed, photographic, or otherwise, without prior written consent from the publisher of Randomly Accessed Poetics, Penhead Press.

Randomly Accessed Poetics, Issue 4: Heart Splatters Into Significance, Edition One was published on 12/21/2013 as an e-Book. The only difference between edition one and two is that all editor notes and photographic additions have been removed, Issue 3 recap and the acknowledgments has been edited and their location has been moved to the rear of the book, and font formats have been altered to look good on paper.

RAPoetics™ Literary Magazine was published by Penhead Press™

CONTRIBUTOR DIRECTORY

CARLA BLASCHKA   9
    Eye Look Skyward at the Dog Park
    Student Loans and Cockroaches
    I found an Orange on Broadway Avenue
    Door Beyond Today

JIM BOGGS   15
    A Study in Gray

GREG BRISENDINE   16
    Addict
    Tattoo

CHRISTINE CLARKE   19
    Before & After
    Operating Instructions for a Trash Compactor

ALFONSO COLASUONNO   21
    The Washroom

TIM COLE   23
    Screams of Silence

LARRY CRIST   24
    The Fallguy
    Progress
    Used Furniture

JIM DAVIS   30
    Lunch At What Was Once The Depot*

DOUG DRAIME   32
    The Frozen Wind Blew

ELIZABETH FOUNTAIN   33
    Goddess of New Orleans

JEANNINE HALL GAILEY   **34**
    Introduction to Genetics
    Introduction to 39

SARAH GAWRICKI   **36**
    Untitled Photograph*
    The Moon

JACK HAINES   **39**
    A Trip to the Psychic
    I Invented That

WILLIAM WRIGHT HARRIS   **47**
    The Agony of Love*

DAWNELL HARRISON   **48**
    The Mirage*

CHRISTOPHER J. JARMICK   **49**
    Letting Go
    Not a Poem About the Divorce

DUANE KIRBY JENSEN   **51**
    Truth About Sunflowers 1
    Bone Dancer
    Quantum Physics
    Truth About Sunflowers 3

ANNETTE KLUTH   **59**
    I am Now

CRAIG KURTZ   **61**
    Rays
    Radio

SCOTT LAUDATI   **65**
    Grit*

CHARLEY MCATEER   **67**
    Someone Is Watching

TERA MCINTOSH   **68**
    Are You Here Yet?

JOHN MCKERNAN   **69**
    Power

SHARON MEIXSELL   **70**
    Fire Inside & Out

DAN NIELSEN   **71**
    Bodwell
    How We Fight

B.Z. NIDITCH   **73**
    Three Cups
    At Summer's End
    Waiting

RAFAEL AYALA PAEZ   **76**
    Vaishvanara / Agni

BRANDON PITTS   **77**
    Zul Qarnain

RAÚL SÁNCHEZ   **81**
    The Measure of our Words

M.A. SCHAFFNER   **83**
    Aspects of Faith Beyond the Toll Road

CAROL SMALLWOOD   **84**
    The Sermon*

MORRIS STEGOSAURUS   **86**
    Asylum

KURT SWALANDER   **87**
    A Letter to America

ANDY WILSON   **89**
    Dear Trickor Treaters

PURPLEMARK WIRTH   **91**
    A Snippet of "Welcome to Club Chaos"

ABOUT THE CONTRIBUTORS   **93**

ACKNOWLEDGMENTS   **100**

ISSUE 3 RECAP   **101**

SUBMISSION GUIDELINES   **103**

MORE FROM PENHEAD PRESS   **104**

CARLA BLASCHKA (2 IMAGES, A STORY, + A POEM)
Eye Look Skyward At The Dog Park

STUDENT LOANS AND COCKROACHES

I asked my friend Merlin the wizard when was I going to meet my tall, dark and handsome and he snapped that while Merlin does get around the cosmos, Merlin never claimed to know the future.

He was cranky. Another lab had rejected his application with the ubiquitous "we have decided to move forward with other candidates who more closely match the needs for this position." He was currently outfitted in blue, in honor of the season. It was B.B. King's birthday, and Merlin was a dedicated fan. I've known him for years. As far as I can tell, after an aunt gave him that chemistry set when he was ten years old, he never came out of the basement.

I told him if he stopped talking about himself in the third person, he might have better luck. He gave me the finger.

I was sitting on a broken down armchair with an Indian bedspread making it respectable, and was playing with the fire extinguisher I kept in my lap. With Merlin it paid to be prepared. We were considering the problem of blowing up the world. Hieronymus, doodling on his sketch pad, was always on the side of the alien invasion, I advocated for natural disaster and Merlin was all for creating a better death through chemical means.

We heard sound, but in our internal world our response to it suffered from a lack of attention. Then we heard clomping. A witch dropped a pizza onto Merlin's spell book and scowled at him, hands on her hips.

"I have been hollering at you for ten minutes. I am too old to be coming down those stairs."

We regarded the wild haircut that always surrounded the toothless face of our constant source of food, Merlin's mother. Then Hieronymus, Henry to his mother, the best socialized of us all jumped up, gave her a hug and kiss on the cheek and lifted a slice dripping with cheese and said:

"You're a life saver. Will you marry me?"

She cackled like she always did when he said that and clomped back upstairs. After several more hours, we all felt we had created a new and fresh approach. We would have an alien invasion, defended by nuclear weapons and various earthquakes and volcano eruptions would occur. Amid all this activity, Earth's surface would simply be vaporized.

Now that we had a plan to get out from under our student loans we felt better. If only we could get a job.

I Found An Orange On Broadway Avenue

We proposed for Witches Abroad on Broadway, a costume.
As a lure to students, orange and black candy.
Dancing at the prom, cell phones caught the ghouls.
This stretch of road was full of cool cats.
Unlucky ones were left on the side as skeletons.
We swept them clear with our broomsticks.

Our guns were not as brutal as broomsticks.
Bristles hid the phallic end, as if in costume,
No flesh, just skeleton.
Like bags of orange and black candy,
They were left, full of calico cat.
Our familiars, our friends, dinner for a ghoul.

They pulled at the ghoul,
In the hands of a witch, danger came by broomstick,
When ghouls snacked on cat,
In their orange and black fur costume,
Tasting sweet, like candy.
They beat them up and down, but they find another skeleton.

Them ghouls come faster, giving birth to others, another skeleton.
Vocalizing desire for black and white, red and yellow make orange, a ghoul,
Howls for student flavored candy.
A witch lays out one, then another with her broomstick,
Removing the face mask and costume.
Them that can, holler their outrage in cat.

Your sex was revealed in orange and black on a calico cat.
Females cooled themselves of sex, unwilling mates to a skeleton.
Once alive, copulating loudly, now in a death costume.
Walking upright, a neighborhood was destroyed by a ghoul.
Neighbors watched, a witch patrolled on a broomstick.
Your students were seen as human candy.

One wife beater had a juicy rind, sweet and soured candy.
At the dance, hors d'oeuvres were made of cat.
Shot forward, it can create a hole, can a broomstick.
Where stomachs used to be, a skeleton,
Death conquers all, no more ghoul.
One, now many properly attired for the Danse Macabre in costume.

I found an orange, as broomsticks cleaned Broadway of cat candy.
In my student costume and human face mask, my path is crossed by a cat.
It disappeared as if it never was, visible only to Death, a skeleton made by ghoul.

Door Beyond Today

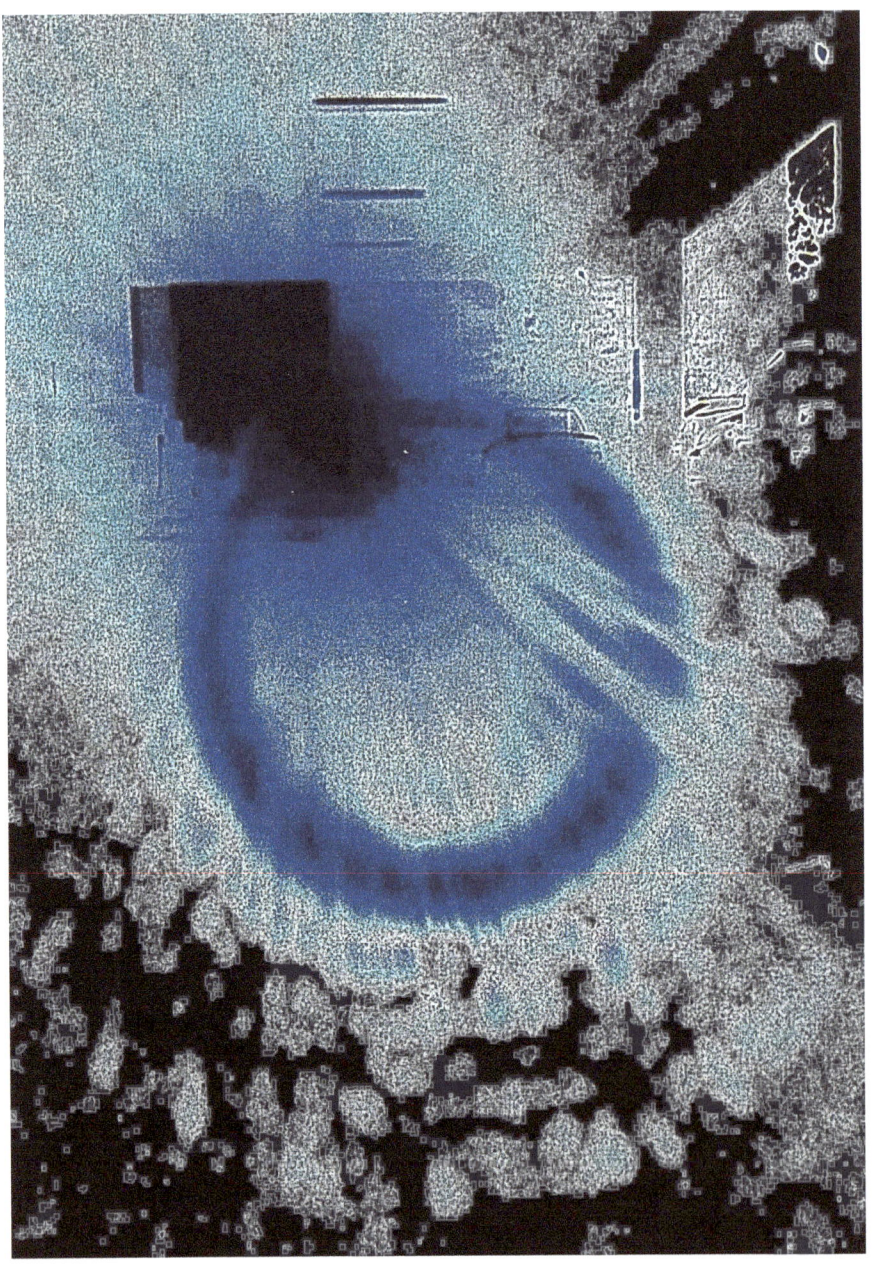

JIM BOGGS
A Study In Gray

Innocent babies wait
with watery eyes and blank stares,
sins and salvation forgotten.
Toothless smiles and open-mouthed sleep
tell the story of the makers of our world:
school teachers, captains of industry,
Red Cross workers, carpenters,
loving mothers, and ne'er-do-wells
in wheel chairs or house shoes
roaming the chaotic halls.
Their small rooms display
grandchildren's art on the walls.
Glancing at every passerby,
looking for loved ones
who brought them here to be nursed,
some expecting nothing but lunch.
Fearing inconvenience
eyes fill with tears when you come
and tears when you go,
crying for reasons they do not know,
staring at "Wheel of Fortune"
in a wet diaper waiting for change.
Matriarchs, patriarchs, brothers and
sisters, waiting like children for the mystery,
ready to enter the mother's womb
only she and the oatmeal are certain.

GREG BRISENDINE (2 POEMS)

ADDICT

I know a man addicted.
Untied from the moorings of reason.
He can't map the path
From rain to puddles,
From sun to sweat,
From flame to pain.

He can't map the path
From the coil of the burner
To the scars swirled on his palm.

His family pleads and cries at each new burn.
Coiled poison stacked on deeper coils.
His family blocks the path to the stovetop
Reminding him about heat
And pain.
Then they watch in horror
Again
As he reaches for the burner
With empty eyes.

Tattoo

I crave the simultaneous sting of 10,000 bees so I can show you what I believe.

I want a tattoo.

But I don't trust myself to believe tomorrow what I believe today.

I believed once that blood was thicker than water and I wanted rivers running red across my skin, but then I was cradled by ocean swells and learned that blood and water both answer to the moon.

I believed once that love conquered all; a Valentine heart with boxing gloves, but lately I slip smoothly down paths of least resistance, shoulders shoofing by granite monoliths that once cried out for conquering.

I believed love was a noun and wanted to diagram it in sentences across my chest, but I think now that it's a verb, in perpetual evolution, so that the ink-frosted donut I present to my sweetheart looks, in just the right light, like global forgiveness.

I want to show you the creak of a wooden mast when I catch giggles in canvas and sail over the precipice past everything I know...like the cover of that Kansas album from 1978.

Those all sound like great tattoos, but who am I to dam the flow of tomorrow's truth by branding today's across my skin?

Up to now I can tell you that: Lord of the Rings is the literature that changed me, Patty Griffin puts my emotions to music, and Calvin & Hobbes showed me the value of friends.

But there are writers, musicians and artists just imagining their truth today, whose work will cause the cells in my body to spontaneously regenerate tomorrow. <sigh>

I don't have enough real estate for what I have left to learn.

So my plan is to come to the end withered and drained, but instead of a preacher at my deathbed; a tattoo artist, ready to document a whole life's learning on my failing flesh.

My last breath will synthesize the totality of my evolution into something graphic – maybe just a single line – the folly of a lifetime succinctly reduced and represented in ink as I cast off.

But my suspicion is that there will be hidden wisdom in the bite of her needle and before the holy tattoo artist has sped me on my way, I'll need a do-over, an asterisk next to the line, or a footnote – aptly tattooed on my foot next to the toe tag – to capture that final truth.

In the meantime I'm more interested in the map to where I'm going than the map of where I've been. So I look for my reflection in the skin-and-ink intersection of other people's tattoos hoping for one that looks like the answer to a question I haven't asked yet. Because the bees aren't telling and drifting is disorienting and some days truth is an anchor that just won't catch until it's written

in blood.

CHRISTINE CLARKE (2 POEMS)
Before & After

It's hot
we're both exhausted,
naked on top of the sheets
still sweaty, breathing heavy
in between sleep
our hands meet
my leg drapes over yours
and I wonder:

Is this the Before
everything was formed
before the breath drew in
and filled lungs,
before matter mattered
before the birds
trees, fig, leaves
Before the apple
the serpent, the sin
the silk of your skin
before the fall

or is this the After?

Operating Instructions For A Trash Compactor

Press <OPEN>

Carefully arrange the love letters
and the sharp tin cans
with the gold wedding bands.

Layer with torn photographs
burnt toast
and bitter orange.

Place heavy objects
like anger and broken china
on the bottom.

Shove in the clotted words you bit back
on lips and tongue.

Hit <START>
Stand back.
The smoking is normal.

Press <END CYCLE>
Wait for steel tongs
to remove the jagged obsidian core.

Remove it
and call it your heart.

ALFONSO COLASUONNO
The Washroom

They come one after another
An endless procession
Like Nazis marching on Poland
Dayglo relics of the seventies
Filled with whole food and scraps
Sometimes they don't empty their trash
It has to be picked off in our line

By the end of the shift
Our stink is nauseating
It rises up silently from their chicken bones and sauces
The conveyor belt always keeps them coming
But the high-powered washer never works as advertised

There's some music on in the back room
Rap (not hip-hop) or what's left of rock and roll
That earnest rock bullshit
We pass three hours' time
Listening to the stars on the radio
And talking about whose sister is pregnant
If we say anything at all

We pass our time like robots
The cup washers
Blasting the soda and coffee with hot water
Those least envied – the dish cleaners
Using soap to get the gunk off of their plates
The easy pricks
Loading the dishes onto the wash line
The lucky bastards
Bringing the trays back for them
The washroom is a place

Different from the rest of campus
There is no privilege here
Only the cries of our distant ancestors
Still longing for a better life
As they cross the Atlantic
And finding out the bitter truth
Their progeny are still their reflections

TIM COLE
Screams Of Silence

What are these forces that move within our lives
That surround our hearts with walls of stone
Detaching us from each other
Depriving us from what we seek
There is a sorrow for which only silence knows
A wisdom only attained from those who's breath has ceased
And by one man's dream of tomorrow
Is one child's past that chooses never to remember
And that wisdom, was better not to be known at all.
This is a dance of thrown paint
A delicate movement in a war of unspoken laws
A competition of will whose end only, is in defeat
And these lies that we sell to ourselves
We whore ourselves only to ignore the truth.
This burning wood with this moons light
They fare far better than the instant fall
A war with no words, wisdom with no life, winters hand embraces us all.

LARRY CRIST (3 POEMS)
The Fallguy

Don't blame god
it wasn't Her fault
it had nuthin' to do with right or wrong
good or evil, you or me, what we said
or didn't say
or how we pray
nothing to do with faith
karma, moral comeuppance, sin
or who was supposed to win

God doesn't look like anyone we know
not Charlton Heston or Brad Pitt
or even Victor Mature
He doesn't sound like James Earl Jones or Ceil B deMille
He never talks to presidents

He doesn't have a favorite town
Mecca, Vegas, Saint Augustine, Katmandu. . .
it's all one to. . .
Doesn't have a sex or even have sex
doesn't have balls or a dick or a cunt or tits or even an ass
doesn't require sugar coated euphemisms
adapts handily to any pronoun—allah them

Doesn't have a favorite team, candidate or party
Doesn't choose anybody over anybody else
one country under. . .
No trust in any currency
Does not control weather
Does not rain on anyone's parade
nor strike lightning when pissed
Gives talent to none

Aristotle, Beethoven or Ricky Henderson. . .
God doesn't give one goddamn about any of it
Does not take offense when cursed
Does not answer mail
Will not return calls

PROGRESS

On our walks around the city
this girl i used to date
would recall
what went where:

That used to be a dog kennel.
That was once a record store.
Over there used to be a Thai-restaurant.

I wasn't as fascinated by the history
as with her ability to remember
She was still in her 20's
but her recall was that
of an ancient elephant

I thought of her just today
seeing a fresh empty lot
something just destroyed
its pieces piled up in a green dumpster
erased from the corner and ready
for the next thing

Last week something stood there
I had walked by it as i walked by now
Whatever it had been was already lost to me

Whatsherface would have remembered

Used Furniture

Why's it called skid row?
Because men on the skid gather there.
Don't women go there too?
Not as often as the men.
Will we see dad down there?
Not today.

She drove her new used car
There was plenty of parking in that part of town
The sidewalks lay wide and empty.
Papers and wrappers drifted by
Pigeons stood their ground
Bottles and cans lined doorways of places no longer open

Where are all the bums?
Shh, don't call them bums.
Hobos?
Hobos live near freight trains.
Winos?
Shh.
Well, what do i call them?
Don't call them, and don't speak to anyone.

I kept my eye out for whatevertheywerecalled
We went in one of the big cheap furniture stores
A slight man with mustache, wearing a tie and no jacket waited on mom
I looked at a wind-up Victrola

Come on, we're leaving.
Aren't we buying any furniture?
Not here.
Why...
Come on.

Back outside i saw a man on the sidewalk
I walked up to him

He wore a hat and when he looked up i saw he had an eye missing
I was going to ask if he were a bum or wino but asked where his eye went?
What? You see it?
He laughed and i saw his eye wasn't all he was missing
Mom yanked me away
I told you not to talk to anyone.

We rounded a corner from the main street
There were 20 to 30 men in the shadows standing, sitting, waiting
Wow, look at 'em all. What are they waiting for?
I don't know, come on.
She would not let go of me now
We crossed to the empty side
and entered another furniture store
A bald guy with glasses and suspenders waited on mom
She continued to hold my hand
The man was showing her dressers
I felt mom jump then move away from the man

I don't believe this.
What, what?
We left the store
He grabbed my behind.
Is that why we left the other place?
He made an indecent proposal.
What's an indecent proposal?
Nevermind. We're going to Sears. They have to be gentlemen there or they lose their jobs.
And then what? They end up here?
It would seem, that or in the used furniture business.

We got back to the car
My hand was getting sore
I saw a man across the street pissing in a doorway
I raised an arm to point this out
Mom pushed me in on her side
He turned as we started the car
He smiled wide and slowly put himself away
His teeth were really white and strong
He was all there

JIM DAVIS

Lunch at What Was Once the Depot

A small bird lands in the brush near the street
after my chicken sandwich arrives and he will not
stop talking to me. Pesto, ciabatta, distracting
clicks and whistles and rustling of leaves. A fly
rubs its hand together, risking its life at the edge
of the spout, where a spot of heavy cream turns
into a small porcelain ewer. There are rules
to language. Ewer seems far too effluent to be
a place for milk. There are rules to the brain and
its placement, its organization of things: Spanish
and English, for example, are stored separately.
I am clicking the back of a pen and tapping it
against my teeth, constantly distracted by the tiny
bird making racket in the brush near the street.
Glowering, I return to my studies when a man
in a camouflage cap asks directions to the train.
What I tell him is mostly accurate. You are almost
there, I say, take a left at the stone staircase, go down,
you'll see a plaque announcing the 1996 landing
or passing of the Olympic torch, churning through
town to Atlanta. Already they are stringing lights
through the trees. It's hard to be nostalgic when
you are never far from home. Grounded, unmoved –
see also – Stagnant, unused. There is no possibility
without risk. The post of every bike rack is shackled
to a bike - that is, grounded to the mobile part
of said equation. Three pigeons on the tinstone
station ledge, and already I am worried
that equation was the wrong word. But it's too late.
The waiter in the Reebok t-shirt has returned
with the bill, and I still have to be at work. To think

that another in the same situation might carve
his name, or near directions, in unrecognizable script
or dip his fingers into a sweet light coffee to stir
the cream and save the fly and slowly sip what's left
past staining teeth and souring tongue, close his eyes
and breathe the subtleties of therapeutic rewiring, muted
wail of a train, wherein whose wake he once set down
some Swedish fish, a plastic comb, his first handful of coins.

—"Lunch at What Was Once the Depot," was previously published by Literary Orphans, 2013.

DOUG DRAIME
The Frozen Wind Blew

The frozen wind blew through
all parts of my life

like some whirling Titanic
iceberg.

Everywhere I went the freezing
followed:

even in July it went to 10 below,
when

her eye lashes grew icicles and
her heart finally froze me out

completely.

ELIZABETH FOUNTAIN
Goddess Of New Orleans

JEANNINE HALL GAILEY (2 POEMS)

Introduction To Genetics

The night before my third brother's wedding,
they go to a bachelor's party, not at a strip club or bar,

but a shooting range, trying out each other's guns,
or renting something bigger, listening to the bang bang

and hitting the bull's-eye. Truth be told, I wish
I could be there too, squeezing the trigger, bracing myself

for the recoil like I did when I was little, back before
we had "shooting ranges," when we just shot into our woods

and didn't use ear plugs or goggles and no one thought
twice about a seven-year-old girl handling a rifle.

My brothers let me ride in the back of their pickup trucks,
occasionally even drive them, put me on the back

of their motorcycles when we were out of eyeshot,
threatened my boyfriends as a matter of course.

In this last night of celebration, our hair turning
the same shade of grey, the light becoming less kind

as we map out our next target, not too distant.

INTRODUCTION TO 39

Every year my birthday comes in April,
with a fickle sun and pollen on my fingers.

I wake up in a field with a scrap of cloth in one hand
and a fistful of wheat in the other. Wheat represents
a blonde fertility goddess fading with the light; the cloth
is the floral print prom dress that still hangs in my closet.

Did you ever think you'd make it this far? Imagined children
in the distance like somber ghosts, taking notes. You have lost them,
your home, the name of their imaginary fathers.
Shades of a different country, forgotten.

In the years close to forty a woman might stop looking
in the mirror. But when I was thirteen, I dreamed of thirty-nine.
Even then my hair turning grey, my blue eyes washing out,
wishing to be taller, older, free as trees in the wind.

In my imagined future I wore pink heels with white shorts;
the future would be full of bookshelves, clean carpet, champagne glasses.

These days I drive fast and play the music as loud as I like.
I am not afraid of the policemen. The shine of water makes me
reckless, necklines more restless.

Come help me blow out the candles. We will eat only the frosting
and put on movies about vulnerable boys standing in the rain,
waiting for us to come out to them, pale and patient as the April moon.

SARAH GAWRICKI (PHOTO + POEM)

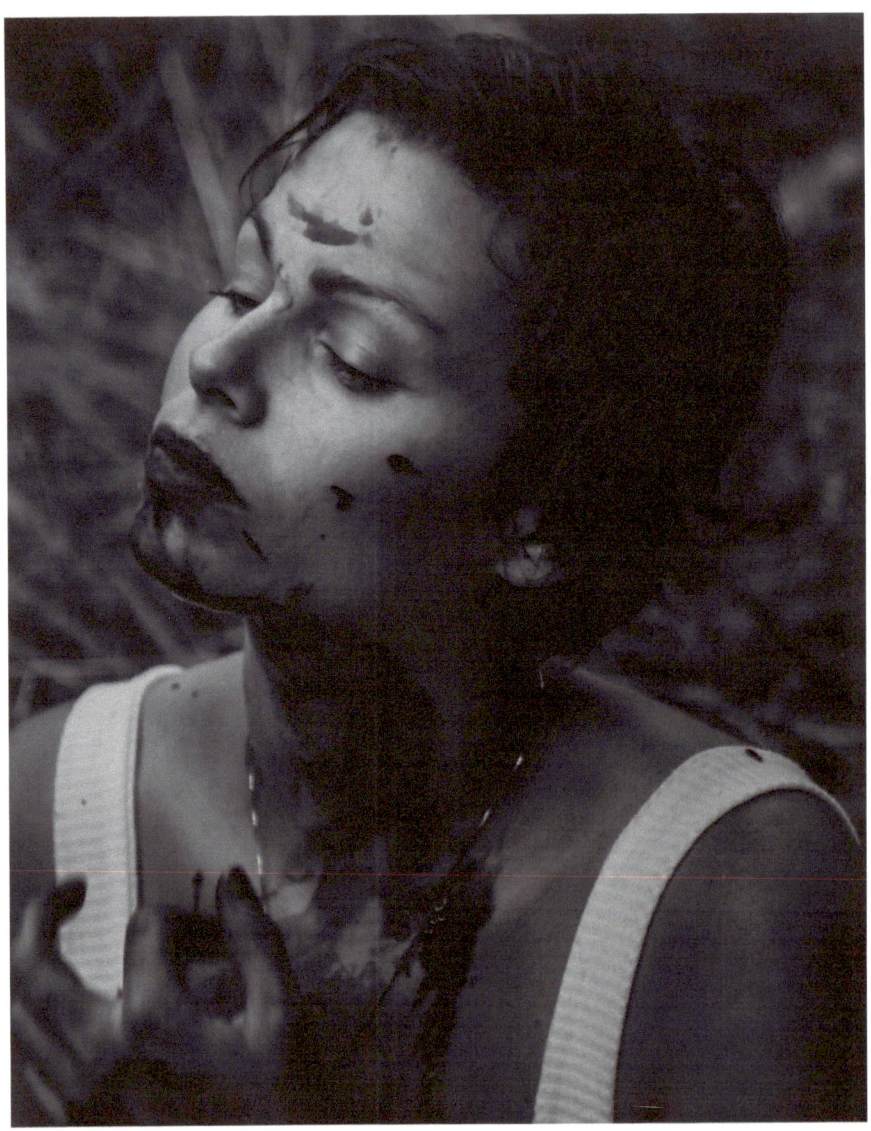

— Photo subject: Sarah Gawricki. Photographer: Erik Ballew. Look up <u>Erik Ballew Photographics</u> to see more.

The Moon

I believe in the moon and its cradle sky. Gravid master: big and effulgent and white, winking— driving all the dogs crazy.

It used to be this way. When no one howled and they all tucked their tailbones between their skin: I spent several nights pouring Everclear into Slurpee cups and lapping at the world's shoelaces. Sitting on the edge of the bay on a borrowed blanket, vomiting up some sort of philosophy about the closing of the day; the way it moved like an itinerant wave that followed me— and only me—everywhere I went. It grabbed me each sunset. "Come here, girl!" it hollered and threw me to the floor. It took the pieces of breath I had been saving for a rainy day when I would finally make a declaration. I'm too dizzy. Wherever I had been standing, I was now wilting. My mouth was moist but most everything else was desiccated. I retold this often to whomever and always myself. The way schizophrenics tell three thirds of themselves to take it easy and the other half is grabbing the window sash and throwing it up and flying away. How many parts is that? There was a glance of sadness or kindness or something else and then a sip. Then my overeager lover attempted to go down on me sixteen different times to prove his might to absent men. I wanted to gulp the last of my rainbow cist and move on but I let him make me moan a couple out before I rushed into the ocean, arms spread open wide just begging to be taken to the place that sharks dine. I wanted to be eaten with force. I wanted to be taken alive.

There were so many of us. All these mad cats and mad old me swimming in subdued psychosis and small talk that had me shaking like a weak shed caught in a thunderstorm. All these sick people and me and no God between us. We found summers that never ended and that seemed better than heaven but we age and we wonder: whose side are we on? You wanted to kill something inside of yourself and you kept naming it my ex. Wait until the stars line your path and you'll see— it's you. You're the only face glowing back. Like a haunted conch shell sitting on some little girl's dresser next to the unremitting twirl of a dancer: it's elegiac twist, pointed shoes, sunken chest, pencil thin lips, little volts that break your coral-colored skeleton in half. She just wants a pretty paperweight and you just want your slimy, little body back. A consecrated beast just learning how to yelp. Breaking your back, breaking your hips and your jaunt to rush up a stake and plant yourself on it. You're out of ideas and droplets of blood and the dirt's giving birth to more maleficent flesh. I'm out tonight, winking like a lunatic, and giving birth to breathing eggs. Pacing the place, listening for the long whimpers of lost wolves. "Come here, boy!" I'm much brighter tonight than I've been in a long time.

I shine like the moon.

JACK HAINES (2 STORIES)
A Trip To The Psychic

"I see you work hard for a living, Senor," her dark eyes gleamed as she looked up from my hands.

I don't really think she was out limb with her statement like she tried to make it sound. My hands were as dry and rough as Mojave Park. La Senora Gomez, the Psychic Palm-Reader knew how to put on a good show. Ambiance will help to reassure the susceptible and her place was chock full of ambiance.

Walking in from the street you would see a small neon sign in the shape of a hand in the window. Printed on the inside of the electric pink outline were the words: "PSYCHIC PALM READER."

As we entered the converted two story house, a bead curtain separated the alcove and the front room. The front room was "lit" by a floor lamp on either side of the room. The lamps must have been plugged into a rheostat in order to lower the output of the bulbs to twenty-two and a half watts each. They both wore faded shades with most of the fringe pieces still attached.

On the right side of the room was a glass fronted case. Inside the case were dozens of apothecary jars filled with dark colored substances both solid and liquid. On top of the case were larger glass jars with what appeared to be various dried animal parts; paws, tails, wings and beaks. All of the jars wore time yellowed labels with Roman Numerals hand printed with red ink to indicate a coded system of inventory control. It had everything necessary to put you in the mood for magic.

On the left side of the room were three overstuffed chairs that sat side by each. Centered on the top of the back of each chairs were white lace trimmed antimacassars, none of them matched each other. The lamp stood in the near corner and ruled over those who would sit below.

Straight ahead was a wall with two doors. In the space between the doors hung a large picture of Jesus, it was the picture of Jesus, palms together, looking up as if he trying to remember where he left his keys. Perhaps he came here to have La Senora help him divine their location and she took his picture for her trouble. The odor of petiole and sandalwood filled the air to the point that for a minute I thought that the picture might have been that of an old English professor I had in college, his name was George.

Below the picture was a pedestal with a statue of Jesus. It was the pose of Him with his hands spread apart. I looked for the caption card that would report that famous quote: "I caught a fish this big!" I always wondered if He was the Patron Saint fishing exaggerations.

I was at the Psychic Palm Reader's studio/shop with my friend DeWayne. I told him that I would accompany him for a reading even though he understood I held no faith in the "Art".

DeWayne was having trouble with his girlfriend, Brenda. Ever since she got her new job as a secretary with the State motor pool, she seemed to be more distant. She kept breaking dates with him and seemed to be letting herself go in the appearance department. DeWayne was emotional and always could read more into a situation than anyone I knew.

"Look at her! She used to be so sexy and wore sexy clothes. Now she wears sweatpants." Because he was almost crying, I agreed to go with him to see the seer.

We sat in the large chairs in the front room and waited for La Senora Gomez. DeWayne sat with his hands on his knees. He strummed his fingers in time with the Mexican music that we could hear from behind the left door. It reminded me that the oom-pah beat of most Mexican tunes is the same as a good German Polka.

DeWayne's eyes were wide but instead of taking in more scenery, he just stared straight ahead, he was practicing his questions to the fortune teller.

"You'll be just fine, DeWayne. I'll tell you what," I said calmly, "I'll go first."

Just then the left door opened, there was no music coming out of the open door. From behind the door was darkness. Into the dimly lit room glided a small framed, white haired woman. Wearing a flowing white dress and a dark brown cross held around her neck with a brown string. She looked like the ghost of a small child.

"Buenos Dias, I am Imelda Gomez. How can I help you today?" She offered her hand, I took it and she led me to the door on the right. She opened the door and I held it open for her to lead the way.

When I entered the room I was impressed, for as dim as the ante room was, this room was fifty times brighter than a normal room. My eyes hurt when I was exposed to the brightness. The walls were covered with layers of white material which defused the light which must have shown up from the floor and down from the ceiling along the walls. The sheet like material obscured the location of walls and even the corners of the room. The floor was covered with a white carpet but the ceiling was a pale blue.

In the middle of this faux cloud was a small round table. A red table cloth touched the floor all around the three foot high, four foot round circle. A high backed wooden chair was placed at three o'clock and another at six.

Missing from this divine look-alike were the things I thought would be standard equipment; no candles, no crystal ball, no gypsy music. In fact there was no music at all from nowhere specifically you could hear wind blowing. When I said I was impressed, I should have said completely impressed. At this point I knew DeWayne was going to be a dead duck. I was a non-believer and my mouth was dry from being wide open for the last two minutes.

We sat in the chairs. She examined my right hand and made her opening statement. I told her she was correct. She smiled a kind knowing smile.

"I know why you are here, mi hijo."

"Oh, really?" I tried not to sound too smug.

"You are a non-believer but you care for your friend. You think because he has problems, he will be taken advantage of by me and by others. You are a good friend. He is lucky to have you. I am impressed to see how much heart you have."

"Thank you. You have a very impressive place here. You see very clearly which is impressive also. What is your plan for my friend?"

"I can tell he has Love Problems. He doubts his love is returned. He is young and needs his love returned, yes?"

"You are very good. How do you know these things?"

"Remember the sign on your way in?"

"What are you going to tell him?"

"The truth, mi hijo, the truth."

"Be gentile, please."

She smiled broadly.

I returned to the ante room. DeWayne's eyes got big.

"It'll be fine, Buddy," I said.

Thirty minutes later, DeWayne returned.

"Well?"

"I'll tell you in the car," said my friend.

On the way back home, DeWayne almost burst. "She was amazing! She knew everything!"

"Are you going to be okay?"

"She told me I was looking for returned love. After I told her my Brenda worked for the State motor pool, she said the same thing happened to her daughter. Not to worry, she told me, she joined the state workers' union. They have meetings every month after work. To ensure a good attendance, the leaders serve pies and cakes. She's not growing away from me, she just growing. I guess it happens a lot."

I Invented That

The ad read: "We hire inventors! Send Us Your Inventions! We Pay Top Dollar!"

That was all it took! That ad caught the big old trout sitting in my chair. That shiny Rooster Tail with the bright red bead, feather and brass spoon flashed in the morning sun light that streamed through the patio door behind me.

"Honey, I'm going to be an inventor!" I told my wife, Ruth. She was going through some e-mail at her desk next to mine.

She had that look she gets when I have a great idea and she can't quite see the big picture. Her head tilted down as she peered over her glasses.

"Remember? Before I retired, I used to invent all kinds of helpful tools that I used around the various jobs I worked on."

That was a fact. Throughout the years I had created small adaptations to existing tools that in some way assisted some specific work process. Because they pertained to different job sites in different years, it was easy for me to cover each of the inventions with the same generic name.

From job to job, across the Northwest, I would be heard shouting to Bobbie, the apprentice, to locate and bring to me a"Jack-U-Later". I always figure that since I invented the tool, I might as well name it after myself.

There were many generations of the Jack-U-Later, some as simple as a wedge, some complex with moving parts like pulleys and levers. Each worked like a charm and each bore the name of its inventor.

"I have a whole box full of Jack-U-Laters in the garage, they are practically new." I blurted out.

"Jack, I don't think..."

"And what about my two ply sox invention, remember? Cotton on the inside and wax paper on the outside to make it easier for old guys to slip on their shoes."

"Well..."

"I know! You're always skeptical of internet offers. This time it's different. It sounds like a real job with a desk and everything and no nudity on my part, unless it pertains directly to the invention."

"Of course."

I called the number in the ad. After talking to Brenda at the front desk, I made a mental note to not mention the Jack-U-Later at the start of any conversation, ever again. She put me through to Brent, the agent, although he sounded more like a salesman than an agent.

"So, Mr. Schmedley, you want to be an inventor."

"No, Brent, I am an inventor. I want to make money on my inventions instead of just storing them in my garage."

"That's the attitude! Here at 'Inventions, Inventions, Inventions' we help you connect the dots to become a first class rich and famous inventor, like that high-tech guy."

"Gates?"

"No."

"Allen?"

"No."

"Jobs?"

"No. Wendell Martin."

"Who?"

"Wendell is one of our clients."

"I'm sorry, I've never heard of him."

"Wendell invented the dot, you know like in dot-com, dot-org, dot-edu."

"I still don't..."

"Well, I can't tell you too much, it's still in litigation."

"Hmmm."

"Anyways, we can take care of you. Do you have an invention?"

"Yes, I do. I call it the Jack-U-Later."

"You invented the Jack-U-Later?!"

"Yes, I did. You've heard of it?"

"Heard of it? I own one!"

"?"

"I bought it when I was in college, I bought the trainer model. I always wanted to meet you and thank you."

"We might be talking about two different things; is it a tool adaptation system for construction jobs?"

"Oh...maybe you're right. Anyways, I'd love to see your version. If it doesn't stretch any copyright laws, we could be millionaires. That's with an

M, Jack."

"You can help with copyrights? I've got questions about how that works."

"It works like a charm. Last year, I took on a client who came out with a whole line of products. He went to China and bought a container full of Chinese merchandise, shipped it home and slapped on his own label and he can't keep it on the shelf."

It seemed we were getting further away from my topic but I thought I would hear him out.

"So anyways, he invented a product name that people can't resist. You've heard of Jesus Brand Products, haven't you? That's my client!"

"Well no, not really."

"You haven't heard of Jesus?"

"Well yes, of course I've heard of Jesus."

"See! Now isn't that a name you can trust? Jesus Brand Shampoo wouldn't burn your eyes. Jesus Brand Ice Cream tastes creamier. Jesus Brand Gasoline will give you better mileage, so you won't run out when you need it, like when you are driving through the bad part of town, you know, where all those Jesus hating illegal aliens live and would sooner knife you as to look at you or Jesus Brand Bullets to put in your Jesus Brand AR-15."

"Oh, so what was the problem?"

"Who said there was problem? We just have to discuss some fine points with the FDA, EPA, NRA and the American Dairy Association. For some reason, the only Chinese import items that didn't contain high concentrations of lead were the bullets."

"No problem with the brand name?"

"With two thousand years of name brand familiarity, nobody took out a copyright on

'Jesus'. I checked."

"Well, I was just looking for a job working in an inventing think-tank where I could work on my ideas and develop products like my two-ply sox."

"I couldn't help you on that."

"What? Why not?"

"There would be a conflict of interest. We represent Jesus Brand Old Guy Sox."

Cover Art Inversion

Cosmology of Photonic Accidentalism
© 2013 by William James Lindberg

WILLIAM WRIGHT HARRIS
The Agony Of Love

the unicorn
    horn somehow warm
white ivory
    piercing
the shape of a heart or a
    hole
eroded into a wall
    of brick masonry by
wind & rainwater &
    love
blood dripping as warm
    as the nude reclining
at mythic hooves or the
    indifferent rays of a
watercolor sun dali
    hung in the sky

—**"The Agony of Love,"** was previously published on **Rays Road Review**, 2013.

DAWNELL HARRISON
The Mirage

i am married to a mirage.
the moon rises under

the meat of your tongue.
forty five years now i have
worked to pull the muck
from your mouth.

still it is all exit signs
leading nowhere.

it is unbearable out here
in the desert having

to endure this intolerable
heat while you dream up
your next big mistake.

—**"The Mirage,"** was previously published by **The Blue Hour Magazine**, 2013.

CHRISTOPHER J. JARMICK (2 POEMS)
Letting Go

I will plant flowers
in the dead man's shoes.
Puncture the heel so
the root can expand
into the soil
as they weather and disintegrate
into the planter on the deck.
But how will my heart wear
if the plants die
too soon?

NOT A POEM ABOUT THE DIVORCE

Signing the declaration of dependence,
on the yacht
left in the desert,
we sailed to the land of 50 percent off--
thanks to solar powered windmills.
Our inventory was shrinking so fast
we couldn't tie the boat to the dock,
so we saw the end of the world
and laughed when the banana's
slipped on the human skeletons.
Then she said, "She didn't understand me
any longer."
I told her to jump,
but she got a lawyer
And we split everything in half.
I tried to tell her 'getting even,
means you haven't gained a thing.'
She didn't listen (she never listened),
So the boat sank
and we fell into the water.

'See. You're no good without me,'
She screamed.
I didn't actually hear her
I was drowning at the time.

DUANE KIRBY JENSEN (2 IMAGES + 2 POEMS)
Truth About Sunflowers 1

BONE DANCER
—After looking upon an untitled painting by Malcolm Liepke

Her eyes bore into me
I feel her weighing my heart,
Weighing my worth.
She examines each scar—
 touches lightly scabs
 too moist to heal.
Discovers holes needing
 needle and thread.

Captured within that dark-eyed gaze
 I am hers - if she chooses me.
I would lose myself
 within the intensity of her passion
I would set the world ablaze
 to see her smile.
I would be her bone dancer
 summoning the dead
 to worship at her feet.

Quantum Physics: *A Quirky Love Story Told In Three Parts, Which Is More About Sorrow And Escape And The Moment A Little Redheaded-Girl Learned To Walk Through Walls After Discovering The Limitations Of A Half-Rusted Machete.*

1} The Exotica of Chaos

His brown-eyes blinked with astonishment
as he witnessed the woman with curly-red-hair
slide through a solid wall,
through solid matter
as if she were a single proton
seeking her own course,
leaving only the sadness of the song she was singing
hanging motionless in the air – waiting
to be plucked and eaten as if it were low hanging fruit.

Within that moment he finally understood
the nature of nonlinear dynamics
    within the construct of a wave.
The method behind the randomness
    of an individual wave contorting
      into a monster-wave,
turning north-shore oil rigs into origami-shaped tinsel;
submerging a nine-hundred-foot vessel
    into the deep-black
before the officer-of-the-deck can inhale one last drag
    of nicotine into his lungs.
These beautiful 'freaks' mock the rules of physics
seducing one to pursue subatomic beauty
within the exotica of chaos.

These surging waves swat clouds.
Clouds that dream only of playing upon the peaks of
    Everest or Annapurna.
Clouds that dream of being worshiped
    by thirsty sunflowers

and millions of open-faced poppies
in high isolated valleys of Afghanistan.

Where poppies eagerly inhale songs
    heard upon the wind,
drink-deep the lyrics-of-sadness
trapped within each water-molecule
that free-falls toward thirsty fields.

    ~ * ~

Filled with his new knowledge - the brown-eyed man
whose jaw is still dropped agog -
starts to pursue that who he thought he had possessed -
steps with bold-confidence toward the wall
that the woman with curly-red-hair
    slipped through with ease.

Stunned - his ears hear the contraction of bone,
his nose shattering into a mammalian accordion -
three-heart-beats before searing pain sends a scream
caroming through-and-out-of his larynx.

A scream that passes through matter.
A scream that makes her eyes smile.

2} The Truth about Sunflowers

Clouds promise moisture to sunflowers
that make everyone smile - except
a little redheaded-girl - who screams at sunflowers
for mocking her with their big-yellow-roundness.

Their incessant smiles silently saying –
in a sing-song-voice of an annoying child:
"Everything is wonderful. Everything is fine.
Everything is yellow and bright and right."

The little redheaded-girl screams
at their yellow smiles
as she hacks them to pieces
with the half-rusted machete
she discovered beneath her father's bed –
next to the crumpled-paper-women
whose naked bodies had been badly soiled.

She kneels upon the happy-faced husks –
now mangled into a sloppy-salad of ooze and fiber –
thousands of sliced-opened-eyes
    continuing to taunt her.

Her momentary revenge fails to ease the pain
of her frayed identity – an anchored cord
ready to snap.
An identity defined by the weight of her tears.
Tears that have evaporated into the air.
Tears that have become clouds
    – free to travel the world –
    – away from her body-arching sobs –

Clouds becoming cool refreshment,
    which nourish the roots of poppies.
Feeding them her mournful-stories
which now nest within each bud
waiting to blossom within the high isolation
of Afghanistan mountain valleys.

In time – the little-red-headed girl learns
to free-fall through earth and lake,
to walk upon the underside of oceans,
to stroll through the rock of mountains,
to bathe in lava as if it were a field
    of red-poppies in bloom.

She learns how to be unbound
she learns to sing the old songs
she learns the best ways to make sunflowers scream.

3} Secret Hidden Within Poppies Tears

Within the poppy fields of a remote Afghanistan valley
appears a red-headed woman who understands
the physics of walking through walls
while singing ancient Welsh-witch songs,
tones that taste like low-hanging fruit
waiting for sharpened teeth to penetrate their core.

Her songs – filled with the wild-beauty
    of unchecked sorrow
become the drink poppies jones for.
Words transforming into liquid.
Liquid seeking its way into petal and stamen.
Liquid embedding her stories within each poppy's DNA,

Liquid waiting to be released into dreams
as poppies ooze latex
that dries into poppies tears.

Her stories lay harbored – waiting to set sail
where tears meet flame –
where lungs inflate with beguiling smoke
that coils its way through the unguarded minds
of those who scoff at the freedom calculus awards,
of those who retreat instead to the safety
    of walls and fences

and the scarlet promise of resurrection.
Those pursuing the wisdom of the dragon –
those searching and failing to discover
    the trail to rapture –
will discover her truth –
the truth of sunflowers and machetes–
They will discover how sunflowers scream –
how they scream with the octave of a fluffy-bunny
at the moment talons punctures flesh-and-bone.
Those who worship the smoke of poppies
will never know unbound freedom
that tastes like low hanging fruit.

Nor the electron-charged kiss of chaos,
nor the mathematical map of the mind
that unlocks the means walking through matter,
nor the bliss of riding a monster wave
    – as if it were a horse

galloping through miles of blood-red poppies.

TRUTH ABOUT SUNFLOWERS 3

ANNETTE KLUTH
I Am Now

A runaway train highballing
No more slowing for stops.

A flash of fire out of
A grease laden pan;
Burning anything in my way.

I HAVE BEEN...

A Mother
Grandmother
Sister
Daughter
And lover to all;
Now exception to none.

I AM ...

Grief
Degradation
Humiliation
Abuse;
Stuffed into a mortar...
Ready
Set
Flame.....

NOW I AM...

The fireworks
You never saw on the 4th of July.

The acrid sulfur smell
Permeating your lungs.
Absorbed in your bloodstream;
Never to leave.

Exhale me on every breath.

Taste my soul in every bite.

I WILL BE YOUR...

Bad dream that makes you awaken
Panting, unsure of where you are.

Forgetful moment;
That made you lose your keys.

I WILL ALWAYS BE...

The runaway train;
To hit your ass.

A grease flame;
To remove your touch from my skin.

I WILL NEVER...

Let my heart love you again.

CRAIG KURTZ (2 POEMS)
Rays

I don't know
the time
or how
much I have
but I'm
sure.
If I still got a
running meter
I'll want these
last rays
of day
with you.

Maybe it's a
malingering cough
or it's where
the train lets off.
The expanse I took
for granted
has an expiration date
and this last
harvest moon
is courting
the coda.
Calling you.

All my life
I've slept in late
and seen my
blood evaporate.
"There will be time"
to save daylight.

If I can
stall
the metronome,
the best sunset
I'll call
all yours.

Radio

I thought of you
with the radio on
and noticed
how many songs
were written
about you
before you
were even
born.

You love
every love song
like the last one
will be your last.
But you always
loved the new one
more than
the last one.

Why would you
care if a song
came and gone.
Good tunes
heal all wounds
and your radio
is always
on.

There's no end
to your hit parade.
There's ever
a carousel
of verses

and chords
all written
just for you.
There's no
favorite;
there's only
diapason.

I had the
radio on
and I
heard it
sing to you.

SCOTT LAUDATI
Grit

they all want to be artists
they change their majors
from psychology
to sculpting
they change later
from sculpting
to economics
their parents say get a job
save money
you can work your art out on the weekends
most give in
get the job
they sleep around in their twenties
they get pregnant
sometimes for love
usually by accident
they get promoted
they become their refrigerator

some stay on
move to the dominican neighborhoods
move to the outer boroughs
keep hustling
always one contact away from the big gallery
thinking they made the sacrifice
art owes them now
one day it will happen

but it doesn't
or when it does
it's just too late
too much time happened

to question, playing
the ultimate gamble
with no chance to return
and get it right
or rewind
and try again

but they bet their life
and the ashtrays never emptied
and the bottles never corked
and they left something behind
good or bad
they wrote their own epitaphs
and the graveyards
and libraries
and art galleries
all filled
because the artist lived
and the artist left something behind.
but whether the dream
was lived out
or sold out
it's hard to see a family
on a blanket under a free sky
every july 4th
or around a christmas tree every december
or taking a picture
with mickey mouse in the florida summer
and argue
that the love that shares your name
is the only art
worth waking up for

        —**"Grit,"** was previously published in **Fjords (Volume 2, Issue 1)**, 2013

CHARLEY MCATEER
Someone Is Watching

TERA MCINTOSH
Are You Here Yet?

On the fall morning I woke still dreaming of you
I glanced in the mirror to see your lips still indented on my cheeks
I imagine you asking me what time it is
But hours hardly matter
When you are no longer here.

I stubbed my toe on the bathroom cabinet
And as I bent over to squeeze it and ease the pain
I noticed your hands still upon my hips

I wonder if your pelican arms might get a better reach for me
as I imagine them cupping mine----While I brush my teeth.

I use the mixing bowl for cereal today
As I know if you are here with me
I might as well eat for three

The morning sun shows my shadow at your height
Yet I still can't reach my closet shelf.
When I leave for the day the door doesn't close behind me like it usually does
I go back
I pull harder
In a distant world I hear you breathing
A soft humming of a sweet bird

On the mornings I wake dreaming of you
I feel like EE Cummings
I carry you with me
I carry your heart with me.
I can see it in the bathroom mirror
Beating back at me.
I carry it in my heart.

JOHN MCKERNAN

Power

When my mother found us on the darkened kitchen floor at midnight staring at the twin slices of Wonder Bread turning slowly from white to brown in the brand new Emerson electric toaster with forks in our hands and an unopened bag of marshmallows on the sleeping bag she knew she had to do something. She sat down on the linoleum floor and very quietly and patiently told us a long story about her Aunt Verna when she was seven years old who poked a fork "just like the one you have there" into the electric toaster to see if it would turn a glowing red color which it did not but instead Aunt Verna was jolted by an electric current so strong that her left eye "popped right out of its socket and landed in a pile of clothes her mother had just brought in to fold."

The toast was delicious and the next morning when we looked up from our oatmeal at the slices of lightning crinkling the black sky we counted to seven to hear a boom rattle every plate on the table and every window in the house. The black cord of the toaster seemed to wag like the tail of some silver cat. My brother would touch the cord and close his eyes tight.

SHARON MEIXSELL

Fire Inside & Out

paper mixing
time one knows
see scorching
fingers page can within
heat feel
Grace words digs
smoke fire tumbling searing
actions pen
All inside Blazing
ink Out Flames
free
Core known embers
Buried Poem

DAN NIELSEN (COLLAGE + POEM)
BODWELL

How We Fight

She slapped my face. For her
it was like riding a bike
down a smooth
winding hill—
feeling the breeze.

I pretended to think
and that's mental illness.

She straddled me
(For her it was like riding a bike ...) like
a blind man identifying
a dead child.

We stopped making decisions
and then made one more.

A place is a thing
that cannot move.

A thing is a place
that cannot stay still.

B.Z. NIDITCH (3 POEMS)

Three Cups

Some nights pass
with three cups of wine
pass my trembling hands
hot as dog days
suddenly falls
over the devil's wharf
filled with hungry feral cats
near the marble steps
of the jazz club
my shoelaces are gone
as an explosion
from my car
reminds me my bills
terrorizing any constraint
of self-pitying misfortune
to plunge us (quickly)
into depression
braying like a lost mule
and makes the serpent
of a malignant attitude
trying play catch-up
with this double minded
blushing poor in the mouth
     of a once gutsy guy
putting my used car
in reverse, like the verse
of impossibilities
not believing this night
as sirens sound
bathing us in sweat
is all due to my expletives
by tasting the French wine
of a skeptical oration
from an enriched Beat poet.

At Summer's End

at whirling ebb tide
an acrobatic dancer
asks for a partner
  a glass harmonica
responds
on an uneasy voyage
climate
changes our field notes
brass band open
in a delectable cadenza
sounding of fragments
A flat arpeggios
swirls the channels
and you play alto sax
with your crushed thumb
to the current improvisations
with high notes of opinion.

WAITING

Waiting for
magnetic

sunshine
on deck

the joker
   meditates
under
the sound system

when a sudden rain
like   pawns
on the chessboard

invades
liquid solitude

sings
its vaporous solo
   over a ditch water
river of sensation

on our trio's recital,
jazz opens
in an open space

and flesh murmurs,

my sax is ready

a firestorm
dissolves
conversations.

RAFAEL AYALA PAEZ
Vaishvanara / Agni

The fire, pair of the universe,
    creates a sun
spilling out flames.

The fire moves towards the center.

The breath is wind
that sings without stopping.
The eyes
caves
that light up
    in a glimpse of clarity.

BRANDON PITTS
Zul Qarnain

lurching in the shadows
     it is my father who will whisper

I will thresh him out
     for I am king in this realm

clutched in my talon
     the ball that paid witness

to the serpent
     sliding between her thighs

tasting mortal juices
     as she writhed upon asian sheets

and like Moses
     I shall ride forth as Oedipus Rex

two horns rising from my head
     to commune with heaven

sons and daughters
     beholden to money

and painted women
     who service my boot

and there were three prophets in the east
     four prophets in the west

their words payed tribute
     to my goat horn crown

and the enormous heap
     that was their temple

shall provide the stone
    for my vast wall

where archers will stand
    manning pots of hot oil

collected from the pits
    where it gushes forth from sands

in my domain
    the Occident . . . to the Levant

where murderous trolls
    push my phalanx forward

and fathers bid for the rights
    to my will over their daughter's bodies

I will take my pick
    one . . . for each mark of the rising sun

and Roxana shall be my bed-whore
    when the others cannot appease my lust

for she is my property
    as I have done unto them

and I will possess her
    like a foreign rock

after I have laid claim to her body
    I will build them a city

where the alter shall be built
    four and twenty cubits

six palms and twenty digits
    dimensions understood by priests

and those who worship Isis
    the sacred whore

but I cannot touch her
    until tribute is paid

and the golden coffers
    will be carried

by slaves
    marching behind my army

and their bibles that do not make sense
    will be added to my collective

as my forces traipse over their fields of grain
    and my generals delegate the storm

but wise men
    will aid in their reconstruction

with canals to move my ships
    and irrigate their crops

and their children shall loiter in vast libraries
    teaching their parents

and the future
    will be ours

for our light will shine forth from a great torch
    seen for nautical miles

reaching beyond the places I have been
    and I will be remembered
for the fire that burns within
    will destroy this mortal body

and keep on burning
    radiating from the tombs to the farthest reach

haunting the Himalayas
    and the Syrian plains of Armageddon

and they will rush to bow before me
    for I am the vicegerent of heaven in this terrestrial hell

heavenly angel
    earthly devil

I am the Kingdom
    and I . . . am money

RAÚL SÁNCHEZ

The Measure Of Our Words
After today's mid-day thunderstorm

I love the sound of thunder!
crushing, distant lightning
striking sound
on some unknown tree

somewhere—

Lighting up the darkened sky
lucky me, I wasn't outside
playing golf, cutting grass
planting seeds

or cleaning the back yard

lightning reminds me
of impromptu vociferous moments
stand up remarks, finger pointing
accusations of events past

which I don't remember—

Like the energy stored away
up in the clouds – a grudge kept silent
stalking,
a predatory approach

waiting to attack

ready to explode when
conditions were just right!
fueled by alcohol
and resentment

brought down from the clouds

deep within the heart and charged
cloudy memories spilled
on this green earth
for all to hear

in silence

M.A. SCHAFFNER
Aspects Of Faith Beyond The Toll Road

Believe in doorknobs and sooner than not
you'll spend all your time entering the room
you just walked into a moment before.
It's an interesting life, always seeking

the next revelation in carpeting,
living room furniture, carpets, curtains,
kitchen cabinets, dinette sets, and lamps,
paintings by starving artists or Kincaid.

You've got to believe in something and serve
an alleged higher purpose than yourself.
I got your purpose here, some godling said,
on the eve of the Null Crusade, the one

that gave us Denny's and Pottery Barn
in the same strip as a sheet metal church
with an aluminum knob like a cross
on a door that opens onto parking.

CAROL SMALLWOOD

The Sermon

  Why did the Church say death was a joyous event because you got to see God but everything at a Requiem Mass was black? I'd always thought bright robes embroidered with birds and flowers like the Chinese robe Nicolet wore when he greeted Winnebago Indians would've made more sense if life was but a preparation for death.
  Vincent didn't speak at first and just surveyed the congregation before lowering his head. I was beginning to be afraid he was overcome with grief until I sensed it was for effect. When you could hear a handkerchief drop, he began slowly: "This morning we have come to honor Walter Alger, a good friend, a trusted neighbor, a public minded citizen, fond relative, a beloved and devoted father to his adopted children." It was like a speech from Julius Caesar—probably the Roman vestments made me think of it. His voice rose after a long pause, when, rubbing his forehead with his index finger, he said: "I had the good fortune to be one of those children. God had a plan for our brother in Christ just like he has a plan for each and every one of us." He extended his arms like the statue of Nicolet in Nicolet Park: "He was God's chosen, the salt of the earth. Walter let his light shine. May it shine as brightly in each and everyone here this morning in this, His holy church." He lowered his arms, looked approvingly at a sniffling Mary Elizabeth. His voice trembled when he said, "Not one of us has failed to feel Walter's light upon us. He let his light shine. Not one of us can have doubted he was the very salt of the earth. The very salt of the earth." I stifled a smile--my brother repeated his own words like the protestant evangelists he belittled. "Yes, my brothers and sisters in Christ, never doubt that God watches over us. He watches over us. He is the Good Shepherd. Yea, our Good Shepherd. We may ask ourselves, 'Why was I not born with wealth, good looks, good health, as my neighbor next door? Why don't I have a BMW (the car he coveted) in my garage, unlimited credit cards, fame and fortune waiting at my doorstep?'" He paused and looked around, then frowned when a baby began to cry. He sighed and bowed his head in pained silence tight lipped until someone left with it.
  He slowly raised his head and gave a smile of forbearance before continuing: "My brothers and sisters in Christ, it is because, God has far better things for you. God gave Walter Alger the opportunity to prove he

was a Good Shepherd when he adopted two young children." Aunt Hester sobbed louder. "What more perfect example of becoming his brother's keeper could there be than when he adopted my sister and when we lost our parents?" With a deeper tremor and a bowing of his head, he said slowly, "He took us in." After another long pause and nodding towards Aunt Hester, he continued as if returning from some long journey: "He has been a generous founder of St. John's Organ Fund and various funds in my diocese devoted to helping needy children as well as the Annual Catholic Relief Fund. A generous giver. A faithful supporter of God's work here on earth." How much of this generous giving had to do with Vincent becoming a monsignor? I heard he was on his way to becoming a bishop. When he raised his arms the folds of his vestments flowed gracefully: "Now, Lord, take your servant, Walter Alger, with you to eternal paradise. Bring your lamb into your fold." Aunt Hester and Mary Elizabeth were sobbing so loudly I could only catch "...good and faithful servant. Heavenly Father, we ask...the beginning of time...."

    I tried to ignore the metallic taste of blood in my mouth. Aunt Hester had often told me that my real father was in Heaven but I was too angry with him for having Uncle Walt as a brother to really believe it. And why should my mother be "with God in Heaven" when I needed her? Aunt Ida often would roll her tongue inside her cheeks making her mouth push forward, and say about her sister, "Your mother was too good for this earth and God in His wisdom took her to Him." Just then I must have muttered something when I jerked because Jenny put her hand on my arm and pleaded with her eyes not to make a scene. I forced my clenched jaw apart to move my tongue around before swallowing to be sure I wasn't swallowing pieces of teeth that must've shattered.

—**"The Sermon,"** by Carol Smallwood is an excerpt from her novel **"Lily's Odyssey,"** 2010.

MORRIS STEGOSAURUS

Asylum

For Dan Rosenberg

Bruised mon(a)stery boy
clumping through
liquor locker rooms,
'braced in lidocaine.
crying in abasement(s),
clutching collar/bone

the truly alien
become asylums

mirrored walls
reflecting (neo]pre[n)e stares
all they'll see is <strike>stops</strike>
<strike>tops</strike>
spots
 & stripes
<striketops
triceratops>

saneitize each
communique before it passes theshold tongue
we keep a tight ship around here,
among other things

KURT SWALANDER

A Letter To America

Dear U.S of A,

I tried to be a patriot.

I ate fried beef bits & tits with pork rectum three times a day for eighty continuous days in my driver's seat, either driving at 75 MPH on Interstate 5, or sitting in the parking lot, ketchup dribbling from my chin.

I bought 4 condos & 6 cars, I was keeping up with the Romney's, now my credit score is fucked and I have developed depression.

Can I make a supplication to you?

All my cyber friends told me I need to chat! Chat! Chat! Until my computer went KA BOOM! So I bought a new one that cost twice as much without even thinking twice.

America, what does it take to be a good American?

I only buy things made in China.
I get my news from National Enquirer.
"Obama is a hollogram,
    California will sink tomorrow!
        We all have aliens in our basements.

Aren't I a pious citizen?

I follow your commandments,

I own guns… from China, and half of them are automatics

There is a militia in each of my condos and they have been shooting others bullet proof vests everyday—we got them from Wal Mart, it was a package deal, we bundled

America, I believe God wrote the constitution.

I know that murder is the fastest way to become a household name.

If I want to take drugs I go to the doctor, give him a condom, then give him my asshole, I slip five dollars in his waistband and get my script,

I can't buy alcohol so I drink two bottles of nyquil every night just for kicks

I bleed red, my skin is white, and I piss blue

I only speak English because one day every other country will be a radiation testing zone.

Let's go America! You know I'm behind you

I voted for Bush three times, his leadership makes me proud and sometimes I shed a tear of joy when he is on the tele

I don't want health care.

America, I have been trying to get a hold of you for 20 years, but you never respond to my text messages; we should meet for a burger and discuss the future, I'm not going to banter, I'm just sayin', I can meet at the McDonald's on 1st, 2nd, 3rd, 4th, 5th, 6th, 7th, or 8th streets, sorry I can't go any further my diabetes will go all awol.

ANDY WILSON

Dear Trickor Treaters

This is an open and sincere apology to all the trick or treaters who come to my door tonight.

Dear Little Shits - and punk kids who are probably too old to be trick or treating.

Here's why you won't get any candy at my house this year.
Why you'll walk away so damn disappointed.

Why you'll come up my driveway, knock on my door, only to have my brother inform you, with his head shaking regretfully, there's no more candy.

There was last night. But not anymore.

You see, him and his fiance went grocery shopping last night, and they bought a big bag filled with full-sized reese peanut butter cups. Everyone's favorite halloween candy.

Except of course your one friend who's allergic to peanut butter, so he trades all of his to you in exchange for your shitty gummy candy.
Which is probably the only reason you let him be your friend in the first place.

I know they bought it, because I was the one who put it away. In the freezer. Yeah that's right, you were going to get frozen reese cups, the best kind.

But you won't be. Not this year anyways.

Because I ate it. All of it.

I came home drunk last night, and I've been pretty stressed lately, and when I get stressed I watch T.V. and eat yummy things.

In my drunken state I totally forgot about Halloween. And I ate all that damn candy while sitting in front of the television until 3 A.M. watching The Shield, a fantastic emmy award winning cop drama.

I didn't think about Halloween, only whether I should swallow the chocolate now, or let it melt in my mouth some more. And about how Vic Maki was going to get him and his Strike Team out of their current mess. He always finds away, that's part of the show, you see.

It wasn't until I woke up this afternoon, that I realized today was Halloween, and we have no candy.

No candy for you.

No candy for your jerk-ass friends.

Not anymore, anyway.

And believe me, it was delicious.

Happy Halloween.

PURPLEMARK WIRTH

A Snippet of "Welcome to Club Chaos"

"Now you're onto the second subject that you shouldn't talk about in polite company," remarked Steve, "Politics."

It was my turn to laugh. "Polite Company? Is that what this is all about? I hardly think that five people naked in a hot-springs is polite company."

It was his turn to look awkward. I raised a finger and drew an imaginary line down the curtain of cloud above me."

"So, what's the name of this spot?" I asked them.

"Lightning Fish Lake," Helice answered.

"That's an interesting name. What's its story?"

"Well, there's a local myth that tells of an eternal struggle between these Lightning Fish and that is what heats up the water."

"What are Lightning Fish?"

"I've never seen one, but there's enough tales of their sighting from mostly way back to give the place that name. I don't know if they're really fish or maybe they're some type of Dragon."

"Dragon, huh? That's an interesting thing to know."

"Why?"

"I have no idea. The thought just struck me as one of those things it doesn't seem essential to know, but which pile up in the long term."

"Like Trivia?"

"Well, kind of the opposite of Trivia. More like Importantia than Trivia, if I might coin a phrase."

"Long live Importantia!" Jeff said.

"Well, I'm out for a bit," Helice said with a wicked wink as she got out of the little lake.

"Me too!" Bettina said and followed her actions.

"It looks like everyone out of the pool!" Jeff said. "Are you coming, Ash?"

"I guess I am. I just want to dry off."

"Then, you will love this." He took my hand and led me out into their pavilion which made my little dome tent look quite inelegant. The parting of the silk panels revealed a sumptuous place indeed: it was an Oda the like of which Scheherazade might have told the stories to save her life or any number of Harems would've lounged in. Rich in tapestries with low tables of wood, ottomans of leather and elaborate glass lanterns tucked within the gathers in the center room and the two other rooms.

"Wow, this is quite the setup!" I looked around wondering how they had carried all this stuff here. They were sitting in the main room on little hassocks and I found a free one for myself.

"There's a bit of a cheat there. You see none of this is real. Yet it feels real and because the lake is here it works even better," Helice said.

"What about these hassocks? Are we just sitting in the middle of the air?"

"Of course," Steve said, "it's my specialty! Do you think that only Kaldera U. knows about the uses of Magick?"

"Well, no! I would expect that it would be a widely known thing."

"Ha!" Bettina laughed at that naive notion on my part. "Magick is the most basic, yet secretive thing that there is. Why do you think that is?"

"I would say that there's loads of people that aren't seeing what's there before their eyes. They're the ones that sleepwalk through everything. I guess it is rarer than I thought to be using Magick."

"Let's say that Magick is scattered like seeds to take root whenever circumstances allow it to flourish again."

"Very nice!" I applauded, "Is that one of yours?"

"Yes."

I then realized that I was completely naked, yet I was warm, dry and at ease with these people. "This is quite the Spell! It must save on the dry cleaning bill."

"Yeah right. Every Summer we take it out and give it a proper wash-down," Jeff said.

"What's it made out of?"

"Pure Dreamstuff that is," he proudly said.

—**"Welcome to Club Chaos,"** is a novel by Purple Mark Wirth that waits for future publication.

ABOUT THE CONTRIBUTORS

Carla Blaschka's particular genius is the ability to take a perfectly ordinary day, give it a twist and make it horrible. One of the greatest compliments as a writer she ever received was being asked what if felt like to find that severed foot. Carla writes by hand, the stories flowing invisibly like ghosts down her arm and onto the paper, her brain only a bowl of cold spaghetti nibbled on by zombies. She lives in Seattle with her imagination and cats past, present and future. She mainly writes flash fiction; sometimes poems tumble out of those stories.

Jim Boggs is a master of the monologue even when he thinks it is a dialogue. Years behind the microphone as a DJ created a lot of one way communication, and his poetry seeks to avoid that fault. Talking about yourself is boring, and in Harlan County Kentucky where he was raised, it would be considered bragging. Life rule: never talk about money or yourself, but it's okay to talk about your grandchildren.

Greg Brisendine (aka Greg Bee) is a poet, amateur actor, advice columnist, budding playwright, and chili chef from Seattle, Washington. His work has been online, in print and on microphones across North America. Greg continues to discover himself in his writing as well as other people's writing.

Christine Clarke was originally from Wisconsin, and has lived in the Seattle area for the past 25 years, where she divides her time between poetry and biology. Her poetry has received awards from the Seattle Public Library and Redmond Arts Council, and has appeared most recently in Clover and DMQ Review. She was a biologist for the Center for Wildlife Conservation, where she specialized in the genetics of keystone species of the Cascadia Bioregion. She was also a columnist for the IBA Newsletter, where she explored the complex relationships between humans, wildlife and nature. Christine is interested in poetry as reflection of our place in the world and as a medium for social change.

Alfonso Colasuonno is a 29-year-old poet and short fiction writer based in Pennsylvania. He graduated from Beloit College with a BA in Creative Writing. His work has been featured or is forthcoming in Gutter Eloquence, Citizens for Decent Literature, Yellow Mama, Horror Sleaze Trash, Pink

Litter, Dead Snakes, and Bone Orchard Poetry.

Tim Cole is a 40 year old writer who has been writing for about 25 years. He feels drawn to write about human conflict, especially emotional conflict. Tim lives in the southern United States and has a wife and three sons.

Larry Crist has lived in Seattle for the past 20 years and is originally from California, specifically Humboldt County (among other places). He has also lived in Chicago, Houston, London, and Philadelphia, where he received his MFA in theatre. He's been widely published. Among some of his favorites are Pearl, Slipstream Alimentum, Dos Passos Review, Floating Bridge Press, Evening Street Review, and Clover. He's been nominated for 3 Pushcarts.

Jim Davis is a teacher. He lives in a world where nothing is ordinary. He is passionate about poetry and painting. He graduated from Knox College with a degree in studio art. He has won several poetry contests and has appeared in print multiple times.

Doug Draime lives and writes in Ashland, Oregon. His most recent collection of poetry, "More Than The Alley," was published by Interior Noise Press. He also has two chapbooks available: "Los Angeles" & "Rock" published by Covert Press.

Elizabeth Fountain lives in Ellensburg, WA, in the heart of the beautiful and diabolically windy Kittitas Valley. Her first novel, An Alien's Guide to World Domination (this book is well written and fun to read), is available from Champagne/BURST Books (champagnebooks.com). You can read more of her work at lizfountain.wordpress.com.

Jeannine Hall Gailey recently served as the Poet Laureate of Redmond, Washington and is the author of three books of poetry, Becoming the Villainess, She Returns to the Floating World, and Unexplained Fevers. Her web site is **www.webbish6.com**.

Sarah Gawricki is an artist from Boulder and the poetry editor of Fat City Review. She has been published in Rogue Zine, Fat City Review, The

Bitchin Kitsch, ArtBomb NYC, Illicit Mag, Milkmade Magazine, The Winter Tangerine Review, and The Altar Collective.

Jack Haines lives with his wife, Ruth, in the Pacific Northwest. He is a retired construction worker who spends his days scribbling stories, bowling, and playing golf. His latest book, Myopic Observations, was published, in 2013, by Rogue Phoenix Press.

William Wright Harris wakes up for the smell of poetry. He is a graduate from the University of Tennessee-Knoxville. His poetry has appeared in twelve countries in such publications as The Cannon's Mouth, Poetry Salzburg Review, Ascent Aspirations, Rays Road Review, Generations and Write On.

Dawnell Harrison has a BA from the University of Washington and has been published in over 60 journals, magazines, and zines. She also has three books of poetry published titled Voyager, The Maverick Posse, and The Fire Behind My Eyes. Penhead Press will publish an e-book of her poetry called, "The Color Red Does Not Sleep," in 2014.

Northwest writer-poet **Christopher J. Jarmick** has been organizing and hosting readings throughout the Puget Sound for 14 years. His latest book of poetry is IGNITION: Poem Starters, Septolets, Statements and Double Dog Dares (2010). He also recorded the spoken word cd (released in 2009) Radio Pictures: Aural Anxieties with Pulitzer-nominated poet Michael C. Ford. A former Los Angeles resident and television producer with credits that include award winning PBS Documentaries, and segments for Entertainment Tonight, Hard Copy and others. Chris has lived in the Seattle area since 1994, he now lives in Kenmore, Washington, and is married to Teresa (together they have 8 kids).

Duane Kirby Jensen is a painter and a poet. His work is published in six chapbooks, and a variety of other publications. Since 1990 he has read and continues to read at numerous venues throughout the northwest. During the 1990's he published Everett's Independent Voice (an arts and entertainment magazine) and The Drifter: A Poetry Journal. He also coordinated the Mill

Town Poets open-mic. And since September 2013, he has been the host of Everett Poetry Nite. He received the 2013 Mayor's Arts Award for Artistic Excellence & Contribution to Everett's Cultural Vitality.

Annette Kluth is a native Washingtonian and a longtime fan of the slam. She has been dabbling in words for her entire life and has performed these verses in many Seattle area (poetry) venues. Her favorite haunts were Red Sky, Through Traffic Molly, Café Messiah, Homeland, Seattle Poetry Slam, and Everett Poetry Nite (to name a few).

Craig Kurtz is a 54 year old man with Asperger's who lives at Twin Oaks Intentional Community. His first record, The Philosophic Collage EP (1981) was reissued by BDR last year. His poetry has been featured in Randomly Accessed Poetics, Out of Our, and Mad Swirl. He is also been a music critic at Perfect Sound Forever since 2003.

Scott Laudati writes. He wasn't sure what to write and then he watched a Ryan Adams interview and Ryan Adams said "yea i write a lot of songs. I know how to play chords so how hard is it to write a song?" He realized he spoke the language he would be writing in already. After that writing was pretty easy.

Charley McAteer is an artist who has his fingers in a lot of pies. As a writer and musician, he is an Alice Cooper type shocker; he can jolt an audience more swiftly than a bolt of lightning finger-banging Gaia from the sky. Charley has performed in many Seattle area venues including Through Traffic Molly, Green Tortoise, Homeland, Works in Progress, and even on the streets.

Tera McIntosh has a Doctorate Degree from Antioch University in Leadership and Change. She is a member of the Pittsburg Passion, a women's football team; and is a co-founder of Young Steel Youth Poetry Leauge, as well as the Pittsburgh Poetry Collective. She has performed Slam Poetry at many venues including Club Cafe, Cannon Coffee, the Shadow Lounge, Antioch University Seattle, Carlow University, and many living rooms and bathroom mirrors. Most of her writings can be found left in the dryer on tumble dry while others can be viewed on YouTube, and some have been published in Randomly Accessed Poets online.

John McKernan is a retired comma herder. He specialized in depleted semicolons and the repair and recovery of derelict exclamation points. He lives in West Virginia where he edits ABZ Press. His most recent book is Resurrection of the Dust.

Sharon Meixsell lives in the State of Washington. Sharon co-authored a poetry book entitled Spirit Rocks with 4 other poets. Her poem, In the Fog was published in Di-verse-city: 2013 Austin International Poetry Festival Anthology.

Dan Nielsen has always lived and will eventually die somewhere in Wisconsin. He manages an art gallery: Gallery B4S, and is involved with the reading series: Bonk! His work has appeared in places you've never heard of as well as Exquisite Corpse, Wormwood Review, Chiron Review, and other of the larger smalls from late last century. Dan Nielsen has also published work in these books: Selected Poems of Post-Beat Poets, Stand up Poetry: The Extended Anthology, and Created Writing: Poetry from New Angles.

B.Z. Niditch lives in Brookline, Massachusetts. His work is widely published in journals and magazines throughout the world, including: Columbia: A Magazine of Poetry and Art; The Literary Review; Denver Quarterly; Hawaii Review; Le Guepard (France); Kadmos (France); Prism International; Jejune (Czech Republic); Leopold Bloom (Budapest); Antioch Review; and Prairie Schooner, among others.

Rafael Ayala Paez (Zaraza, Guarico, April 24, 1988). Degree in Education, Language Arts mention the Universidad Nacional Experimental Simón Rodríguez (UNESR). Founding member of the Municipal Writers Network of Zaraza. He has published in literary magazines in your country, of South America and Europe.

Prolific novelist, poet, lyricist, and playwright, **Brandon Pitts** is the author of the poetry collection, Pressure to Sing (IOWI), the play, Killcreek (IOWI –

2013 Toronto Fringe), and the novel, Puzzle of Murders (Bookland Press). In 2011, he was selected for inclusion in the prestigious Diaspora Dialogues as an Emerging Voice and has been widely anthologized.

Raúl Sánchez is a Seattle Bio-Tech technician, eschatologist, colletic, prosody enthusiast, hamartiologist, translator, DJ, and cook who conducts workshops on The Day of the Dead. He was featured in the program for the 2011 Burning Word Poetry Festival in Leavenworth WA. His most recent work is the translation of John Burgess' Punk Poems in his book Graffito. He has been a board member of the Washington Poets Association and is a moderator for the Poets Responding to SB 1070 Facebook page.

M. A. Schaffner has work recently published or forthcoming in The Hollins Critic, Magma, Tulane Review, Gargoyle, and The Delinquent. Other writings include the poetry collection *The Good Opinion of Squirrels*, and the novel *War Boys*. Schaffner spends most days in Arlington, Virginia or the 19th century.

Carol Smallwood's books include Women on Poetry: Writing, Revising, Publishing and Teaching, foreword by Molly Peacock (McFarland, 2012) on Poets & Writers Magazine list of Best Books for Writers; Divining the Prime Meridian (WordTech Editions, 2014); Bringing the Arts into the Library (American Library Association, 2014). Carol has founded, supports humane societies.

Morris Stegosaurs is a wordsmith and performance poet. You can find him on YouTube, other places online, and now at select book sellers. Go to Amazon.com and get the book "Zebra Feathers," it is a collection of his best work published by Minor Arcana Press. Morris currently lives and writes in Seattle.

Kurt Swalander is a product of his travels. With the intent of absorbing every sensory experience, he hopes to create a new form of the literary vision. He has completed his first chapbook and hopes to publish by January 2014.

Andy Wilson is a northwest native, poet, performer, writer, e-sports enthusiast, and modern day Ad-Man. He's the author of: How Ugly Ads Make Millions, Advertising Made Easy. Performs frequently in Everett, but sometimes in Bellingham and Seattle too. Follow on Twitter: @AndyWilson22.

PurpleMark (aka **Mark Wirth)** courts way too many Muses: Chocolate-Making, Costuming, Millinery, Photography, Painting, Drawing, Novel-Writing and Poetry. In College, he was the Art Director for the MSU Literary Annual for 2 years and an issue of Scimitar: Illustrations, Layout and some Poetry. In the Seattle area, he worked on Mythos in a like manner and provided additional photography as well as short stories.

ACKNOWLEDGMENTS

First off I want to thank all the contributors. If not for your hard work, I would not be able to put this art and writing collection together!

I want to give special thanks to Duane Kirby Jensen and Carla Blaschka. For without Duane's suggestion of creating a print edition and offering up his poetry venue —Everett Poetry Nite— for a release party, this magazine would not exist. I also give thanks to Carla, because she helped me in the final hour of the submission review process. After a while all the poems and stories start to mush together. They begin to appear equally as good and or equally as bad. Carla helped me narrow the selection pool down to a more manageable lot. And she also helped me mask out the first 8 page numbers of the print edition. MS Word, in all its user friendly presets, is a fucking whore to use for any purposes other than commercial or office applications.

The other important people I want to thank are my mother Lucie Lindberg, Aaron Dietz, Priya Keefe, C. Albert, Larry Crist & Christine Clarke (for being good friends), Jack Haines and B.Z. Niditch (hopefully I will get to meet you both in the future), Greg Brisendine, Christopher J. Jarmick, Annette Kluth, Charley McAteer, Tera McIntosh, Sharon Meixsell, Dan Nielsen, Brandon Pitts, Morris Stegosaus, and Purple-Mark Wirth.

Lastly, I wanted to acknowledge the Seattle writers community. For without that crucible, I would never have been birthed into the writer/artist that I am today. Seattle is the homeland of my heart and I will ever be grateful for her guidance.

ISSUE 3 RECAP (A WORD COLLAGE)

Monsters Have Blue Eyes

"Are you okay," he asked?

I looked away
haunted
A meaningless count of numbers
jumbled inside [my] head
[If I entomb the memory
under a litany of fractions
sometimes it dulls the pain]

A pale sun shines
shuttering [the fragment into a moment]
Music boiled and foamed
The trailer park reminds [me]
Faces contort like sun-stained mushrooms

Guilt crests my brow
I imagined [callous hands]
[and] the caress of frost clambering [between legs]
Childlike, not knowing what to do, I collapsed
I spend hours kneeling down on the floor
shuffling through scraps of paper
[I uncovered] a dozen books on how to breathe

I saw a bird seated on a tree alone
[He had blue eyes]
[9/10, 7/4, 1/3, 1]

"There are ways I keep falling,"
I answered, "I am not here…"

NOTE: Words, Lines, and phrases were lifted from the following Issue 3 contributors: **monsters have blue eyes**, No Longer by Morgan Collado; **"are you okay," he asked**, Iambic Pentameter by Tim W. Boiteau; **I looked away**, Paperbird by Linda M. Crate; **haunted**, Hunger by Mike Berger; **a meaningless count of numbers**, Iambic Pentameter by Tim W. Boiteau; **jumbled inside its head**, Elephant by Allie Coker-Schwimmer; **A pale sun shines**, 3rd West & Republican by C. Albert; **shuttering**, Cold by Mike Berger; **music boiled and foamed**, Wrong Life by Alex Damov; **the trailer park reminds**, Worlds Within Worlds by Elizabeth Fountain; **faces contort like sun-stained mushrooms**, What Time Does the Train Arrive at Station Desperation by Doug Draime; **guilt crests my brow**, Locked by Linda M. Crate; **I imagine the caress of frost clambering**, Already by Holly Day; **childlike, not knowing what to do, I collapse**, Fascination by Alex Damov; **I spend hours kneeling down on the floor shuffling through scraps of paper**, Slam by Nate Depke; **a dozen books on how to breathe**, Villanella for the Old World by Colin Dodds; **I see a bird seated on a tree alone**, Evening Serenade by Jason C. Ford; **There are ways I keep falling**, The Fallen by Tim Cole; **I answer, "I am not here,"** In the Cold Absence of a Church by Holly Day.

In this word collage, I changed pronouns, modified tenses and added or removed suffixes in order for everything to fit together into a smooth narrative. All words and lines in brackets are my own.

SUBMISSION GUIDELINES

Randomly Accessed Poetics accepts poetry and prose of any genre, including rants, essays, flash fiction, and short stories. RAP also accepts photo art, collage, and comic illustrations. Please send your images and scans (at least 600 dpi) as JPEGs. Keep prose works under 1500 words. And for poem lengths, anything that could be read (or performed) in three minutes or less is preferred.

If you're interested in contributing to the Randomly Accessed Poetics online literary e-zine and the biannual e-magazine, you are invited to send 2 - 5 pieces (preferably unpublished) to rapoetics@penhead-press.com.

If you prefer the old-fashioned way, you can mail your poetry, prose, images, & illustrations to:

Penhead Press
PO Box 115
Willamina, Oregon 97396-0115

MORE FROM PENHEAD PRESS

You Can Find These Penhead Press e-Books at the Amazon Kindle Store:

Randomly Accessed Poetics • Texture of Words #1. Features work by Gale Acuff, Carla Blaschka, Larry Crist, Margaret Elysia Garcia, Tere McIntosh, B.Z. Nidtch, and many others from around the world.

Randomly Accessed Poetics • Paint Darkness Into Day #2. Features Kyrsten Bean, Matthew Brouwer, Dawnell Harrison, Heather Parker, Frederick Pollack, Purple Mark, Changming Yuan, and others.

Randomly Accessed Poetics • Sifting Through Raw Words #3. Features Matthew Casey, Morgan Collado, Holly Day, Elizabeth Fountain, Dion Loubser, Jesse Minkert, and more.

Randomly Accessed Poetics • Heart Splatters Into Significance #4. First Edition. Features the same writers' and artists as in the print edition.

Coming Soon:

The Color Red Does Not Sleep. Poetry by Dawnell Harrison. Cover art by Dion Loubser. Penhead Press Chapbook Series #1

Randomly Accessed Poetics • Antiphotonic Illumination #5. Sarah Gawricki will be on the cover. Projected publication date 6/24/2014.

In The Soup: Demented Recipes 2009 — 2014. Flash fiction by Carla Blaschka and photography by W.J. Lindberg. Second e-book edition Penhead Press Chapbook Series #2.

www.ingramcontent.com/pod-product-compliance
Lightning Source LLC
Chambersburg PA
CBHW042309150426
43198CB00001B/17